WRITTEN BY ROBIN STANLEY

ILLUSTRATED BY STEVE HARPSTER & TERRY JULIEN

ISBN 0-7847-1808-3

12 11 10 09 08 07 06   9 8 7 6 5 4 3 2 1

Standard
PUBLISHING
Bringing The Word to Life™

Cincinnati, Ohio

I can be a good sport! Being a good sport means trying to be like Jesus all the time! So I'll obey when no one's looking,

hear my coach when he is speaking,

work real hard when I am learning, and be ready
to do my best!

Whatever you do, you must
do all for the glory of God.
—1 Corinthians 10:31

I'll be an example to my friends, show them how to be a team.

I won't be selfish with the ball—

The goal's the same for one and all!

When we play together as a team, everyone wins! Go team!

Love one another and work together
with one heart and purpose.
—from Philippians 2:2

I won't cry when I strike out. I did my best, and that's what counts!

If a friend's a little scared of falling on the run, I'll be like Jesus—cheer him on and shout out loud, "Well done!"

I'll keep my cool when I am tempted to really be upset.

And even when we lose the game, I'll shake hands with every player!

Be humble, thinking of others as better than yourself.
—Philippians 2:3

So, whether I'm an athlete on a team,

or enjoying a family run,

I will choose to be like Jesus, and I'll have a lot more fun!

*Hold to the truth in love, becoming more
and more in every way like Christ.
—Ephesians 4:15*